T0370521

# LOOKING FOR
# LOVE
## IN ALL THE WRONG FACES

KELLY ANN

WESTBOW
PRESS®
A DIVISION OF THOMAS NELSON
& ZONDERVAN

WestBow Press books may be ordered through booksellers or by contacting:

WestBow Press
A Division of Thomas Nelson & Zondervan
1663 Liberty Drive
Bloomington, IN 47403
www.westbowpress.com
844-714-3454

All Scripture quotations are taken from the Holy Bible, NEW INTERNATIONAL VERSION®, NIV® Copyright © 1973, 1978, 1984, 2011 by Biblica, Inc.® Used by permission. All rights reserved worldwide.

ISBN: 979-8-3850-1608-2 (sc)
ISBN: 979-8-3850-1609-9 (e)

Library of Congress Control Number: 2024900087

Print information available on the last page.

WestBow Press rev. date: 3/12/2024

*Dedicated*

to the Love of My Life

*Jesus Christ*

# CONTENTS

CHAPTER

## Self-Esteem and Self-Worth

LADIES, ARE YOU CURRENTLY IN AN ABUSIVE relationship or have been in the past? I am here to tell you that you do not have to be battered or abused. There is a man, named Jesus that will fill all your hopes and dreams. He is the One you can run to when your heart is breaking and no one else seems to listen. We do not have to live our life as a victim anymore. I am finding more men today lacking the respect for women. And guess what? It is partially our fault. Do you think wearing revealing clothing and extreme eye makeup reflects Jesus' image? Are we looking more Christlike? We all need to pursue purity. After all, we are created in His image. What happened to simplicity and our natural beauty, ladies? Wake up! The money making businesses that are promoting our fashions, makeup, and fragrances are getting rich while the image of modern women today are being demoralized. True beauty is within our spirit and our soul. We do not have to look like the models in the magazines trying to improve what God has already given us, beauty inside and out!

He has also given us talents and gifts that many of us have not tapped into yet.

So ladies, shouldn't we have our focus on our Lord Jesus Christ rather than trying to get the attention of men? He can provide all we need and ever want in a companion. That is where we find true contentment, in the loving arms of our LORD and Savior. No man can fulfill all our wants and desires, because the Lord didn't design them that way. Following all of the LORD's creations in seven days, His first disappointment was discovering Adam did not have a helper. The LORD took one of Adam's ribs and made woman. They became one flesh, they were naked in the garden and they were not ashamed. Genesis 2:20-25 Before the sinful act of eating the forbidden fruit, Adam and Eve both relied on the Lord, it was perfect. However, when Eve found the fruit appealing and she desired knowledge, she not only took a bite, but she offered it to Adam also. That sin branded all of mankind with a sinful nature and the serpent was pleased with the results of his tempting schemes.

So tell me what would really improve a woman's confidence and self-esteem? I know the Lord loves us so much that He would want us to go to Him with all our problems, so He could comfort us. "the sheep hear His voice; and He calls His own sheep by name and leads them out." John 10:3 When I was a young girl, I thought if I had a good man in my life, I would be happy forever! I honestly believed that all men were good and they would treat me the same way I treated them. I stated earlier that no man can fulfill all our wants and needs, but God can; if it is within His Will. Just think what it would be like if He provided all our desires; wouldn't we become self-sufficient and probably bratty. Would we ever have enough? Would our desire be to want more and more material things and less and less of our Provider? When I look back on my life, it bothers me to think how I catered to my previous husbands and how they treated me in return. Yes, I have been married more than once and shamefully say that I allowed them to be abusive mentally and physically to me. We had children to raise, or rather I raised them. And I really tried to be a good mother and wife, but nothing was ever good enough for them. It is strange to say, the harder I tried to make the marriage work, the worse it became. Getting married again was not any better. In fact, it was worse than the previous marriage. It was eight years later that I remarried. Besides the abuse, he was a habitual liar, porn user, woman chaser, and a thief. Oh yes, he had another woman on the side, and married two months after our divorce. He lead me to believe that he cared about his aging mother and portrayed to be such a good Christian man. That was so far from the truth. Can any of you relate to what I am saying? Please do not misunderstand, I am not an advocate for divorce or leaving your spouse. Honestly, I had dreams of having my 50th Wedding Anniversary. I am in favor of Christian counseling for both parties to humbly seek the Lord for His guidance. I am quite a bit older now and realize now that life is too short to waste it away on a miserable life and suffer the bad treatment from others. Believe it or not, we truly are The Lord's Masterpieces; He truly made us beautiful inside and out. (Genesis 1:27) Ladies, if this sounds familiar, my heart goes out to you. I feel your pain and the Lord wants you to know that He is there with you and for you and I can honestly say that time spent in prayer on your knees will heal all wounds.

God's greatest blessings are waiting in the bough for all of us! We just need to ask for them. Seek and trust Him in everything. He will amaze us with the plans He has for us. (Jeremiah 29:11-14) "Are you seeking heavenly treasure or have worldly values sidetracked you?" (In Touch Nov. '21, 10) "How lovely is Your dwelling place, ...My soul yearns, even faints, for the courts of the LORD." Psalm 84:1-2. "Hear my prayer, O LORD God Almighty; listen to me, O God of Jacob ...look with favor on Your anointed one. Better is one day in your courts than a thousand elsewhere." Psalm 84:8-10a (chorus in Matt Redman's song— "Better is one day in Your Courts Better is one day in Your house Better is one day in Your courts than thousands elsewhere." "O LORD Almighty, blessed is the man (woman) who trusts in You." Psalm 84:12 "Hear, O LORD and answer me, for I am poor and needy. Guard my life, for I am devoted to You. You are my God; save your servant who trusts in You." Psalm 86:1-2

Is Satan continuously saying things in your head that you are not worth anything and that you will never amount to anything in life? That is Satan talking to you. Remember how the serpent enticed Eve in the Garden? Are you willing to give up your soul for a little attention or companionship, that you will take anyone that comes along who will notice you? Do you get online and seek the love of a male that you do not know? It is disturbing that prostitution and human trafficking is at an all time high. If your self- image and self-esteem is that low or you know someone that is in abusive situation and they need immediate help, call

Women's Protective Services at (806) 747-6491. There is also another good program for women who are struggling to get their life back on track, but it takes time to go through the application process. That program is called the New Legacy and they can be reached at (806)749-7078. I highly recommend both of them because I have been involved with them personally. I call myself a "people-pleaser" and that is not a bad thing, but I did not make the necessary boundaries in my relationships. Therefore, I was taken for granted and the more I tried to please the men in my life, the worse it got. Yes, there were fights and I was one who didn't back down to defend what was right in the truth. There were a number of injuries and one trip to the Emergency Room that went unreported to the Police. And the Police were called out on numerous other occasions, but I had to protect the man in my life, for the sake of our children and our family. Our Lord and Savior loves us deeply and He NEVER intended for us to be beaten or beaten down. Find someone who is a Christian and ask them to pray for you and show you how to pray, if you do not know how. When you hurt, He hurts too. When you cry, He cries too! We are His children, His beloved children, created in His image. He is always with us, He sees everything, and there is no reason to hide. He is our refuge and strength in our time of need. "I cried to my God for help. From His temple He heard my voice; my cry came before Him, into His ears." Psalm 18:6 He also answers our prayers. It maybe "no," it maybe "yes," and it could be "wait." But it is always in His timing, not ours. Remember, He knows our past, our present, and our future—the future we are totally unaware of. Also remember that He made plans for us before we were even a thought. "Before I formed you in the womb I knew you, before you were born I set you apart" to do great things. Jeremiah 1:5 So you do not have to be perfect, you just need to be obedient and have faith He will do what He promises in His Word. Whether you realize it or not, we are children of the Almighty God, King of kings and Lord of lords. What more could you ask for in a relationship? That alone should remove all self-doubt and low self-esteem. Jesus didn't come to earth to condemn it, but to save it. He carried our sins and hung on the cross so we could have eternal life. We were given freedom, not free to go on sinning, but to repent. To turn our life around so we can see the One who truly loves us. Don't get me wrong, family members try to show their love, but Christ Jesus is always there with open arms, offering compassion to the grateful and the ungrateful. He is drawing you to Him with grace and mercy and wanting to shower you with His blessings. "Seeking God is a lifetime pursuit" "diligently seek Him-day by day through His Word and prayer. Forfeiting this great blessing is a tragedy." "Seeking the Lord simply cannot be hurried. It will cost you time and energy, but the rewards of knowing Him intimately are worth any sacrifice. Are you willing to make the necessary effort?" (In Touch Nov. '21, 11)

Do you have self-control so you can stand against Satan's schemes? "You did not choose Me, but I chose you and appointed you to go and bear fruit-fruit that will last." John 15:16a This verse reminds me when Esther was chosen to be the next queen for King Xerxes. She was chosen because of her beauty and later found favor with the king. King Xerxes was unaware that she was a Jew and Haman wanted to destroy all the Jews because of his jealousy for Mordecai, who happened to be Esther's cousin. Haman pressured the king to sign a decree and seal it with his ring, making it official and unable to reverse it. When Mordecai heard of this, he went to Esther and pleaded with her to go to the king, even if it meant the death sentence for Esther. Only if the king extended the gold scepter to her, could she approach him in the inner court. Mordecai's message to Esther: "' Do not think that because you are in the king's house you alone of all the Jews will escape. For if you remain silent at this time, relief and deliverance for the Jews will arise from another place, but you and your father's family will perish. And who knows but that you have come to royal position for such a time as this?'" Esther 4:13-14. More of the story, Esther had Mordecai gather the surrounding Jews to fast and pray for three days. Then Esther went to the king and he did extend the scepter to her and asked her request of him. The story goes on with a good ending and it demonstrated the blessings that the Lord has for us if we are obedient and faithful to Him. I am finding out the closer I get to the Lord, I feel the peace that surpasses all understanding. "Sing to the LORD, you saints of His (His godly ones); praise His Holy Name. For His anger lasts only a moment, but His favor lasts a lifetime; weeping may remain for a night but rejoicing comes in the morning." Psalm 30:4-5. The Lord and I shared those tears, but He was faithful with a brand NEW day with sunshine and the promises that He will always be with me. "God allows you to experience brokenness so you can die to self, because it's self that limits the eternal influence you have with others. As you relinquish your need for control, you are able to experience the transforming life of Christ." "That resurrection life that Jesus lives through you is what attracts others to Him and ushers in true power and eternal fruitfulness. But you have to let go and trust Him." (Jesus, Our Perfect Hope, 325). It is true, we can only serve one master and I serve the Lord Jesus Christ. And I hope that is true for you also. This has made such a difference in my life to follow the Lord's Will rather than my own. Yes, I tried it numerous times to do things on my own and failed miserably. "You cannot accomplish in the flesh what only He can do through His resurrected power. But for Him to live through you, you have to give up. So stop fretting. Release control of the wheel and let Him drive." (Jesus, Our Perfect Hope, 324). Think about it, wouldn't you want that same resurrected power that Jesus had at the grave and when He ascended to heaven? I certainly do.

CHAPTER

## Fear of Being Alone

DO YOU HAVE THE FEAR OF BEING ALONE THE REST of your life? I suppose I felt that way when I allowed smooth-talking men sweep me off my feet. Again, I use to believe all people were good and they had the same morals that I had. Wrong! The Lord allowed me to find out what men are capable of doing and thinking. It is true that not all men are alike, just like all women are not alike. We are all unique and have been given different personalities. There is ONE BIG question to ask yourself before you consider a relationship with someone. It's not do we have anything in common? No, the BIG question is, are we equally yoked? What that simply means is, are we both believers in Jesus Christ? If one is not a believer, don't go into a relationship with the thought you will change him eventually. That only happens in rare cases and it would not be wise to put yourself thru that misery for any length of time. It is incredibly important to have balance, to believe in the same things. For example, what does darkness have in common with light? To make a relationship last over time, two people need to share their thoughts, their laughter, their tears, and hopefully their common goals with one another. Otherwise, you end up becoming roommates, instead of husband and wife that God intended. Another issue I need to address. Cohabitation doesn't really work out in the long run, I know I tried it and regretted it. To be honest with you, deep down you lose all respect for each other when you give your body to another without the marriage vows and the commitment to one another. We should know that God designed intimate relationships in a beautiful and respectful way. This was Jesus' reply to the Pharisees, " 'At the beginning the Creator made them male and female, and said, For this reason a man will leave his father and mother and be united to his wife, and the two will become one flesh. So they are no longer two, but one.' " Matthew 19:4-6a. Also in Hebrews 13:4 "Marriage should be honored by all, and the marriage bed kept pure, for God will judge the adulterer and all the sexually immoral." You see that same judgment would apply to me as well. But I have been saved, forgiven of all my sins, and washed clean by the blood of Jesus. I have given Him my life and He has control of the steering wheel and I am anxious to see what He has planned for me next. My life has always been an adventure, but now I have a travel agent.

When I think back in my previous marriages, I felt all alone most of the time because I didn't feel that agape love from my mate. Now that I am divorced, it is okay to be single. I will never be alone again because I have my Lord and Savior with me and in me for all eternity. That is my hope and prayer that you have that same relationship with the Lord. And should you cross paths with another lady that is hurting that you give her comfort, the same comfort the Lord gave you. I have been delivered because of His grace, His mercy, and His love. Since God's plans are different for everyone, it is important that we seek His will for our lives and we must be flexible. The Lord wants us to be ready for those twists and turns on the road that He leads us on. Don't fall for the lies and false promises men say just for the sake of not being alone. I fell into that trap. I was so caught up in my husband's needs, I slowly drifted from my Lord and Savior. It is true, you cannot serve two masters at the same time. **You must choose.** Who is your master right now? If you are in an abusive relationship, I pray the Lord will open your eyes completely to see who really loves you, cares for you, and provides for your needs. I am not asking you to leave your spouse or significant other, but to place Christ first in both of your lives and He will direct you through the storms and calmy seas. I say it again, we should not expect a human to take care of all our needs, they are not equipped to do that. That is Jesus' role of provision. "Jesus tells us that we must read His Word, listen to the Holy Spirit, and incorporate His truths into our beliefs and our lives. When we do this, He says, it is like building a house on a rock-a solid foundation. When the rains and storms of life happen (and they will), the world mocks us or tries to tear us down for our beliefs, but our faith will withstand the pressure." "Jesus is our rock and foundation. We must guard ourselves against things or ideas that are not grounded in Biblical truths lest we build on sandy soil that will fail us." (Journey, Nov. '21, 20). "Outside are the dogs, those who practice magic arts, the sexually immoral, the murderers, the idolaters and everyone who loves and practices falsehood." Revelation 22:15 "... and all liars—they will be consigned to the fiery lake of burning sulfur. This is the second death." Rev. 21:8 Paul warns us of the "Godliness in the Last Days" in 2 Timothy 3:1-17. "Even though Jesus is God's Son, He learned obedience from the things He suffered." But understand, the process of growing your faith is suppose to be challenging. This is because when you have to choose the difficult path—when you must make painful decisions or you simply cannot imagine how the Lord could work things out for your good, it cements your commitment to Him. Obeying God in the tough decisions readies you for both His assignments and His great blessings." "Thankfully, you have a Savior who understands your pain and fears completely, and He's committed to leading you faithfully. So obey no matter what the cost and trust Him." (Jesus, Our Perfect Hope, 361). "In repentance and rest is your salvation, in quietness and trust is your strength." Isaiah 30:15. "Yet the LORD longs to be gracious to you; He rises to show you compassion. For the LORD is a God of justice. Blessed are all who wait for Him!" "You will weep no more. How gracious He will be when you cry for help! As soon as He hears, He will answer you. Although the Lord gives you the bread of adversity and the water of affliction, your teachers will be hidden no more." Isaiah 30:18-20. "The moon will shine like the sun, and the sunlight will be seven times brighter, like the light of seven full days, when the LORD binds up the bruises of His people and heals the wounds He afflicted." Isaiah 30:26. This reminds me of the story of Job. Job went through a great deal of torment and lost everything. However, at the end of the Book of Job, all of his sisters and brothers "comforted and consoled him over all the trouble the LORD had brought upon him." "The LORD blessed

the latter part of Job's life more than the first." Job 42:11b-12a
Job was obedient to the Lord and the Lord knew he would be
faithful when Satan asked Him if he could sift him as wheat.
"Job's suffering was on account of his righteousness, not because
of his sin. Job's suffering was for the sole purpose of silencing
Satan and glorifying God." Life does not always make sense, but
God has a plan for everyone of us! God is truly our anchor in our
storms. "Your relationship with Christ opens the door to every
blessing the Father has promised in His Word and provides all
the resources you will ever need. Jesus is the reason you can have
an unshakable, eternal hope that everything is going to be okay,
regardless of the situation." "So no matter what you are facing
today, don't think of it in terms of your strength or knowledge.
Instead, consider what Jesus—the all-powerful all-wise Savior
who defeated sin and death on your behalf—can do. Certainly,
He is the anchor that will always hold you steady, no matter how
severe the storm can be." (Jesus, Our Perfect Hope, 3) People
believed the coming Messiah would bring a military revolution
and eradication of Roman rule. However, as we know, Jesus came
for a totally different purpose. He came to reestablish the intimacy
with God humanity lost in the garden of Eden—to be 'God
with us' " (Matthew 1:23) "The main message of Christmas is
that God wants more for you than simply making your earthly
life more bearable. He gives you His light, His life, and His
freedom—He gives you Himself!" "So today, stop seeking things
from the Lord and just enjoy the true Gift, the greatest Gift:
Immanuel—God with you. Think about all that really means
and praise Him for His grace." "We have the choice to partner

with God's loving intentions or resist in doubt and fear, but God will not leave us. Because of God's faithful love endures forever. (Psalm 138:8) ...even the deepest wounds and the most twisted hearts can be rescued and redeemed. Lord, help me to not get in the way of the purposes you have for me." (Journey Nov. '21, 23) "So stop focusing on what you don't have and begin to praise the Lord for all He's already given." (Jesus, Our Perfect Hope, 131) Lord, guide me to contentment today. Help my eyes to stay focused on You and the good You bring into my life." (Journey Nov. '21, 27) Remember, with Christ in your life, you will never be alone again! Jesus, You are my rock and my foundation. And that is called:

Deliverance

For He will give His angels orders concerning you
to protect you in all your ways. Psalm 91:11

CHAPTER

# Comparison is a Joy Stealer

DO YOU KNOW THAT COMPARING YOURSELF WITH other women is a joy stealer? It "tries to take what God freely gives us: holy confidence, freedom to be who He's made us, and unconditional love that heals our hearts." (June 25 devotional) I know that it is a natural instinct to look at other women and mentally ask yourself, how do I measure up to her? But the Lord made you absolutely perfect in His image. Actually, consider yourself His masterpiece, similar to a Rembrandt. You wouldn't want to alter his paintings because they are worth a fortune. Now consider yourself worth a fortune, priceless! Make that mental note every time you look in the mirror and you will see yourself differently. And STOP looking at the magazines with envy and jealousy. With today's technology, you might be shocked to know that those pictures in the magazines may not match the actual models they used. Why not be satisfied with what you have been given and seek the Lord's Plan for your life? The money-making companies that I mentioned previously want you to desire their products in makeup, hair products, and diets so they can sell you more and more products. They know if they can make you unhappy or discontent with the way you look, they are there with the latest and greatest products promising to make you absolutely gorgeous! Don't fall for those gimmicks, you are already beautiful inside and out. The Lord created us in His image and He doesn't make mistakes, because He is infallible. Our bodies are the temple of God and He resides in us and we reside in Him. Ladies, we have an incredible inner beauty that cannot and should not be compared to other women. If we kept that thought in mind, we might take better care of ourselves with the resources we already have at our disposal. Who knows, we might be happier with the simple things of life and have a lot more money in our pocket. Shhhh! don't tell those big money-making businesses that they can go somewhere else! Ladies, what would joy or contentment look like for you? What would make you really happy? To be rich, travel all over the world, a multi-million dollar home, luxurious cars, etc? "Are you seeking heavenly treasure, or have worldly values sidetracked you?" (Nov. '21 In Touch, 10) Would you be willing to sell your soul in order to obtain those material things? Then consider what the apostle Paul told Timothy: "Command those who are rich in this present world not to be arrogant nor to put their hope in wealth which is so uncertain, but to put their hope in God, who richly provides us with everything for our enjoyment. Command them to to do good, to be rich in good deeds, and to be generous and willing to share. In this way they will lay up treasure for themselves as a firm foundation for the coming age, so that they may take hold of the life that is truly life." 1 Timothy 6:17-19. That life, the truly life that Paul was talking about is eternal life. There are only two choices: heaven or hell, nothing else. Jesus Christ is truly my life and He has promised to be with me and in me for all eternity. Without Jesus, there is no hope. If you deny Him, He will deny you and you will face judgment all alone and be sent to the fiery furnace for all eternity. Now that should help make the right choice easier. By choosing Jesus, you are given the same resurrected power that He has, by just asking for it with faith. Since material things are fleeting and they do not last forever, it would make sense to choose Jesus over everything else that the world has to offer.

I love this passage where Paul is praying for all the saints (those who believe in the Lord Jesus): "I keep asking that the God of our Lord Jesus Christ, the glorious Father, may give you the Spirit of wisdom and revelation, so that you may know Him better. I pray also that the eyes of your heart may be enlightened in order that you may know the Hope to which He has called you, the riches of His glorious inheritance in the saints, and His incomparably great power for us who believe. That power is like the working of His mighty strength which He exerted in Christ when He raised Him from the dead and seated Him at His right hand in the heavenly realms." Ephesians 1:17-20 My desire is to share that same prayer for you, that you would allow the Lord Jesus into your heart and let Him take control of your soul. That is the most important decision you will ever make in your life and you will be so glad you did!

CHAPTER

# Father Figure

RESEARCHERS SAY THAT LITTLE GIRLS WHO didn't have a strong father figure in their childhood go on into life looking for that same love and affection in other people. Well, I can say that is true for me. My dad was a very good man, but probably worked too hard to provide for his family. He took that responsibility seriously and he worked 18 to 20 hours a day. During my early childhood, he would go to church with the family, but he would be so tired and would fall asleep during the sermon. My mother would then pinch his arm to wake him up. I guess that is when he started working on Sundays, just like any other work day. When he did come home in the evenings I would already be in bed and he would be gone before I got up for school the next day. So you see, I was not able to see much of him until I had my own car. He owned a service station and the service was what made it so special. And the gas prices were very competitive. When I was a sophomore in high school, he started renting small motorcycles and I was just enough of a tomboy to want to ride them. What was fun for me became a nuisance to my Dad. Since

I didn't have my driver's license yet, I couldn't leave his property. I kept running over the bell in the driveway and he looked up each time, thinking it was a customer. Again, I want to say my dad was a good man, but he was a man from a generation that didn't say, "I love you." It wasn't till his last days on earth that he told me he loved me. That meant so much to me to finally hear those words.

Looking back, I believe I would have had a little more confidence and self-esteem if I heard him say that earlier in my childhood. In addition, my mother was always condescending and I could never please her, no matter how hard I tried. That reminds me of the story about Joseph in the Bible? He had brothers that resented him because their dad favored Joseph. He went through numerous trials and persecutions, but the Lord rescued him and delivered him in a way that only the Lord could orchestrate. Joseph was eventually placed in charge of the king's castle and when the famine swept through the land, he extended his forgiveness and love for his brothers and family. He could have had them killed for the treatment he received from them earlier. But he truly loved them and wanted to take care of them. He also understood that it was all in the Lord's plan. It isn't an exact comparison to my life, but I was the youngest of three girls. There was a four-year gap with the sister next to me, and I captured Mom's attention when they were off to school in those early days. It did not help that I was cute and petite and she was a little chubby at the time. I recall one upcoming Thanksgiving and a newspaper photographer asked to take pictures of my mother and I in the kitchen making pies. Yes, the picture ended up in the newspaper for the whole town to see. My sister was so jealous and later admitted in her adult years that she tried to loose me on several outings with the family. Later when I was older, I didn't find favor with anyone, but then I found Jesus while I was in High School. The Lord had other plans for me and it was the Lord who prompted me to write this book. He wanted me to share my story and my experiences to save others from having the same heartaches that I had endured. It is true that life doesn't always seem fair at times, but God promises to always be there with us, every step of the way.

I now want to share a lesson that Sue Jones, my Life Group teacher taught one Sunday, "On The Guidance Of The Holy Spirit."

> "There are two things I have learned over and over through the years: (1) Christians must pay attention to any 'check in the spirit' they have and (2) they must wait for God's Peace. We are spiritual beings on a human journey, not human beings on a spiritual journey. It is our spirit that lives on with God when this body is dead. Above all else God is concerned about our spiritual growth. When Joseph was thrown into the pit by his brothers and sold as a slave to a passing caravan, he must have felt that God had forgotten him—and yet it was all part of a bigger plan to get 70 Jewish people out of Canaan and place them in Egypt where they could grow and thrive under Joseph's protection as prime minister. Everything that happens to a Christian is part of a bigger plan.

The 'check in the spirit' is God's spirit talking to our spirit and giving directions.

But it's **a small voice and hard to hear**. Only the tenderhearted can stay in tune with it. Whenever a Christian gets a check in the spirit and ignores it, the heart gets a little harder. It's like drinking coffee. People who drink coffee enough and get use to it can drink coffee so hot that it would scald the throats of most people. Their throats have been conditioned to take it. So it is with the heart. The more we ignore the checks in the spirit, the more we don't notice them anymore. As for peace, it is the ultimate test. Satan has so much power that he can counterfeit almost anything God can do—except give us **peace**. Only God can give peace. Satan can even make us think we are in love. Have we known people who thought they were in love but something about the other person gnawed at them on the inside? The attraction was there, but the peace wasn't.

> [She just described me. Ouch!] We must go with peace. Unfortunately, God doesn't give us much more to go on than His Word, a check in the spirit, and His Peace. While we work to stay tenderhearted and sensitive to the still small voice, we can take comfort in knowing that—like Joseph—God doesn't make us stay in the pit forever. Where-ever there's a pit, there's a caravan on the way."

And do you know the story of the prodigal son? A young man

asked for his inheritance and it was granted from his dad, so he went off and spent it all foolishly, trying to make it on his own. While he was starving and penniless, just the thought of being home with his family became a comfort. So he returned home humble and ashamed of his poor choices. But to his surprise, his dad welcomed him with open arms and prepared a celebration because of his return. His brother did not understand the reason for celebrating with a feast. After all, he stayed and worked hard with his dad while his brother was off having fun. He did not understand that his adventurous brother has seen the light and was no longer lost in the darkness of the world. He repented of his sins and his dad forgave him, just like Jesus forgives us. We have such a loving Father that He sent His only Son to die on the cross for you, for me, for all of us. He willingly took all our sins so we could have freedom and life for all eternity. In Jenna Lucado's book, "Redefining {beau*ti*ful}" a daughter's relationship with her dad is determined by:

> the way she looks at herself
> the way she looks at others
> the way she looks at God

A healthy father/daughter relationship can build self-esteem, confidence, and "love-worthy." I am sorry that I missed that during my childhood and my late teens. At the time, I honestly believed I would find a young man that would love me and we would live happily ever after. Well, I married a man that I was in love with, but his ambitious pursuit put us in poverty twice and I just couldn't see my baby starve. We didn't have the money to wash her diapers or put gas in the car. So I left and went back to my hometown to raise my daughter. Suddenly I realized that I was a single parent with all the responsibility of two adults and trying to make ends meet. Yes, it was rough and I would not recommend it to anyone. I married again ten years later to a man that was physically and emotionally abusive. We had two boys and I was determined to make it work, regardless of the fights. Looking back, I realize that was not a good situation for me and it was not a good environment for my children. I really didn't feel that I had any options and I stayed 18 years. Oh how I prayed that the Lord would get me through each new day. Until one morning I woke up and the Holy Spirit told me this was the day to leave. Because of my husband's anger issues, I was afraid and didn't want him to come after me with the kids nearby. So I packed them up and took them to my parents' home and I went to a shelter. It ended up in a divorce and with time it all worked out with God's grace and provisions. Well, it did until I was swept off my feet once again and married again. I will share that relationship later on in the book, but I will tell you that each relationship was worse than the previous one. I can honestly say that my biggest downfall was having a big loving heart and would fall right into Satan's trap every time! It is a crying shame that I will never ever celebrate a 50th Wedding Anniversary like my parents did. Now this brings me to another lesson that I want you to really think about. It is from my teacher, Sue Jones, titled:

### "Circle of Unmet Expectations"

"Unmet expectations disappoint us and we begin to focus on what we don't have. It's not about what happens to us, but what happens In us.

How we respond determines how soon we will receive our blessings. Obedience produces blessings.

True faith always produces hope, contentment, and joy."

And the see saw illustration on the next page is titled, "The Will Is The Key." You are either in Satan's world, allowing him to control your body and emotions that leads to death OR you are in God's Word and allowing the Holy Spirit to direct your mind and spirit and have eternal life. **What is Your Choice?**

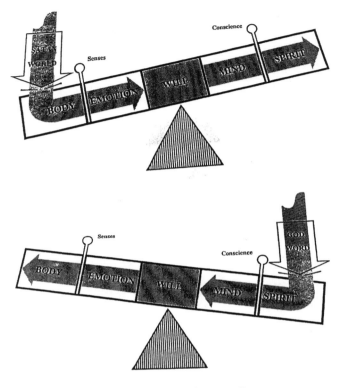

**"The Will Is The Key"**

Right now, The Lord is everything to me. He has opened my eyes to the truth that I really am beautiful inside and out. I am a child of God and I belong exclusively to Him. He has healed my wounds and scars and has shown me His plans to follow Him in the work of Women's Ministries. It is okay that I will never be married again, but I know who I belong to now. He loves me and promises to always take care of me. He wants me to share my story of Hope so that your eyes will be opened to the Creator. He wants you to know Him intimately, because He loves you more than you can ever imagine. Once you have a relationship with the Father, everything will fall into place by His design. I mistakenly allowed the men in my life to takeover mentally and spiritually. They also physically abused me, so please do NOT let that happen to you. When I do not understand, I trust His Heart. The Lord promises hope and provides the love you are craving inside. My earthly father did love me and he is gone now, but I will see him again one day. And I have a Heavenly Father forever and ever. Amen.

CHAPTER

## To Love and Be Loved

LADIES, DO YOU DESIRE TO LOVE AND BE LOVED in return? There is someone who is waiting to hear that from you with open arms. Yes, it is Jesus, our Lord and Savior. He Loves you so much that He took on your past, present and future sins and paid that sin debt in full! You will never have to face judgment the same way that non-believers do. They will face a fiery hell for all eternity, while you face judgment with blessings, based on what you did for His kingdom on earth. Please don't get me wrong, it isn't works that get you to heaven, it is God's grace and your obedience. If you have not asked Him into your heart and acknowledge that He died and rose again, paid your sin debt in full, and that you trust Him in faith, then do it **now!** He will welcome you in His loving arms and He promises to be with you forever. How long? Forever!

Have you heard this song, "**Who I Am**" by Blanca? If not, the chorus goes as follows:

"I'm running to the One who knows me, Who made every part of me in His hands, I'm holding to the One who holds me, Cause I know whose I am, I know who I am, I am sure I am Yours— Fearfully—Wonderfully—Perfectly—You have made me."

That is a beautiful picture of God, our Father, wrapping His loving arms around His precious child, you! It is time to give the Lord Jesus your life, your all to Him. He has done everything to prepare a place for you in heaven. In John 14:2-3 tells us, 'In My Father's house are many mansions.' 'And if I go and prepare a place for you, I will come again and receive you to Myself; that where I am, [there] you may be also.' His loving arms are stretched out to you, do you feel them? Do you want the love and joy that was meant for you long before you were born? You are His Masterpiece! He doesn't make mistakes, but sadly we are the ones who reap the consequences from making poor choices. But Grace is found in repentance and it leads to righteous living. There is no sin too big that God will not forgive, except denial of His Son. So trust Him now with all your heart and you will be set on a new adventure; one that is beyond your wildest imagination. The Christian life begins now and it is a lifelong experience. The more you study His Word, the deeper and more intimate your relationship grows. You will feel the peace that surpasses all understanding. You will feel the freedom you were meant to have, instead of the bondage you may be currently in. Your fears of Satan's attacks are muffled with God's protection. Yes, Christians will suffer persecutions at one time or other, but God stands before us, in us, and behind us. He protects us. I would rather be on God's side of the battlefield than against Him and His mighty forces. He promises to be with us through all our trials and tribulations. He truly loves each and everyone of us! So what are you waiting for? It is time to give Him your heart! Below are the lyrics of a song that really touched my heart while going through the pain and needed God's comfort. Oh I wish you could hear the music that goes with it. And you can, look for "my grandmother's prayer" CD on the website, russmurphyministries.com

### Beauty for Ashes

by Russ Murphy and Bill Gammil

Though you have seen your dreams turn to sorrow
Though there are times when you don't understand
Jesus is there with hope for tomorrow
He'll dry your eyes with a touch of His Hand.

**Chorus**

God will give beauty for ashes
Joy instead of mourning
Praise for your burdens, laughter for pain
If you are willing to trust God above
He'll mend your Broken Heart and fill it With Love.

Cold winds may blow the storm clouds surround you
Feeling so lost and in need of a friend
Jesus is there, His Love all around you
He'll give you strength to start over again.

russmurphyministries.com

CHAPTER

# Forgiving Yourself and Others

DO YOU HAVE TROUBLE FORGIVING YOURSELF? DO you have trouble forgiving others? Forgiveness is a tall order when you have been deeply hurt by others. Have you asked for the Lord's forgiveness? I hope you know that He will forgive you, no matter what sin you have committed. Remember, the only sin He will not forgive is denying His Son. Do you also feel so deeply distressed that you have trouble forgiving yourself? Whatever you have done and you feel remorse of that sin, you are on your way to repentance. Seek the Lord's Word in Psalm and Proverbs. Read those love letters as if He is speaking directly to you; and He really is. He wants you to run to Him with your problems and share your joyous times with Him. Do you have a quiet area that you can get away from the world's distractions? If not, find one. Even if it is a closet, you need a place where you can pour out your heart and He will hear you. He is your Father, your Abba Father, your Daddy. He is your Comforter and your Counselor. In other words, He is your Go To Person, not just when you need a shoulder to cry on. He wants to hear from you every day. He wants to hear your praise and your thanksgiving when He has blessed you with many provisions. He wants to know what you think of the sunshine, the rain, and the beauty around you. He wants to visit with you and consider Him to be your best friend, yes your BFF. If that sounds odd, try it! You will not regret it and you will be so glad you did.

Let's get back to the old sins that you have committed and you can't seem to shake the guilt from your conscience because it just keeps replaying in your mind. "Most people don't set out to sabotage their future, yet it can happen anyway because of their ignorance, rebellion, or blatant disregard for God and His Word. The course of one's life can be derailed by foolish errors in judgment and future consequences can be disastrous." "We're more likely to make unwise decisions when extremely hungry, angry, lonely, and tired." "The acrostic H-A-L-T-signal to us that it's time to pause and evaluate our decision-making." "Impatience and strong desires can also lead us astray and blind us to potential consequences. That's why we must learn to make decisions by using a long-term perspective instead of focusing on what is immediately in front of us." (In Touch June '22, 7) I know from my own personal experiences when I was off track, I made terrible decisions on emotion and definitely without regard to the Lord's guidance.

Looking back over my life, I recall that rare but wonderful feeling when anyone paid any amount of attention to me. I'll give you a little background. I grew up in a small Methodist church and the sermons and teachings were based on "love one another because God made us all." That part is true, but I guess I wanted to believe that everyone had the same kind and loving spirit as God. Wrong! That was a major erroneous thought. The definition of erroneous: "wandering; straying; deviating from the right course." Boy, that is an understatement! Okay, was I ignorant or just naive? But I truly had a true loving heart for others. Do you know anyone like that? Or maybe I am describing you too? I tried to look for the best in people and overlooked their sinful nature; not believing anyone could ever be a liar, cheater, womanizer, abusive, and a porn addictive individual. That just described my last and final husband. I fell right into his prey, like a hungry vulture. Yes, I ignored the red flags waving in my face, just hoping he would change and realize one day that he had a real jewel in me. I also chalked up his bad behavior as imaginations on my part and just wanted to please him more than ever. As my focus grew more on the men in my life, I now see that my relationship with Jesus Christ deteriorated. They just used me and were incapable of loving me for two reasons. They didn't know how to love anyone and they certainly didn't love themselves. They lacked respect for me and did not have any relationship with our Savior. As a result, we were not equally yoked either, a subject matter that needs to be preached in more churches today. In 2 Corinthians 6:14, "Do not be yoked together with unbelievers. For what do righteousness and wickedness have in common? Or what fellowship can light have with darkness?" I must have missed that verse in the Bible and it is such an important one. To be honest, I really thought the Lord was with me at the beginning of those relationships. Or did I just want Him to be and ignored the red flags? Those red flags were not my imagination. Hindsight tells me they were the Holy Spirit's nudging in an attempt to get my attention and I just pushed Him away. I was so caught up in the excitement that someone, anyone, was actually interested in what I had to say. The truth is they were working on a devious and evil plan to hurt me. I cried out to the Lord like David did in Psalm 27:12, "Do not turn me over to the desire of my foes, for false witnesses rise against me, breathing out violence." When Satan is tempting you, remember this:

> Sin will take you farther than you wanted to go, keep you longer than you wanted to stay, and cost you more than you wanted to pay!

> There is no sin so great, no past so painful, no need so deep, that we cannot bring it to Jesus. No problem so small that He cannot be bothered. What a God we serve!

I must confess, I have made several bad choices in men and I didn't know the Lord's plans for me at that time. However, He blessed me with 3 beautiful children and 5 grandchildren. I am so proud of my children for what they have accomplished. Each one has their Masters Degree and a job that will allow them to live comfortably. However, I am not happy with the bad choices they are currently making because of their dad's influence. Yes, there was violence, both physical and emotional abuse during my marriages. Trips to the Emergency Room and the police were called out in attempt to change their behavior. Because of my devoted love, charges were not filed and I covered for their bad behavior. Consequently, they did not learn any valuable lifelong lessons and the abuse continued until the divorce.

To be honest, I am still in the healing process and that is why the Lord laid it on my heart to write this book. He wanted me to share my story and my life with you so that you will heal too. But in order to do that, changes need to be made. The changes have to start with you. In order to improve your situation, you must make those changes and you know deep inside what needs to be done in your life. If not, then first seek the Lord your Creator to help you with those changes. Life can be difficult if you try to make it on your own and it was not meant for you to stay in a miserable rut. If you are lost and you feel the darkness all around you, you can find your way out. There are Christian counselors and pastors that are waiting to help, but the first step is to ask for the Lord's divine help. Seek and trust in the Lord for the peace and comfort that you have not felt in a very long time. Seek and trust in the Lord with all your heart and He will give you the desires of your heart. We no longer have to carry the guilt of sin because we have been washed clean, but only if you are a believer. Our sins were nailed on the cross with Jesus. But first you must believe, pray, and spiritually listen to the Holy Spirit in order to give you the guidance and the encouragement you need for your life. It is uniquely different for every individual. Ungodly actions flow from sinful thoughts and attitudes. Yes, that is definitely a true statement. These things can be changed only as our mind is renewed by the Holy Spirit. As we spend time each day in Scripture, the Spirit transforms our mind and strengthens our inner being. But when we neglect God's Word, we leave ourselves open to the influence of the world and our flesh, both of which opposes godliness. Then, if we try to change our behavior without adjusting our thinking, we'll find ourselves doing precisely what we want to avoid. (Romans 7:15) I want to share something that the Holy Spirit has recently prompted me to do. When I would get flashbacks of the bad things that happened in the past, I use to get angry. Now I stop and say out loud, **I choose to forgive** (and say the person's name that would come to mind.) Charles Stanley wrote it so well in a devotional on Feb. 2, (Jesus, Our Perfect Hope, 56)

## "Not Condemned"

> Yes, God sees all the painful things in you and He has allowed them to surface so you can be set free of them. That is what His grace is all about. He is not content simply forgiving you of sin; He wants you to be completely liberated from its destructive influence on your life.

Actually I do not have a choice to forgive; the Lord demands that I forgive others just like He forgave me of my sins. In order to have eternal life with the LORD, I must follow His example and His commands. "Jesus said we should love God with all our heart, all our soul, all our mind, and all our strength." (Mark 12:30) "It's a lifelong process that requires learning God's thoughts and adopting them as our own. Then, as the Spirit develops within us the mind of Christ, our actions will become increasingly holy." (In Touch June '22, 14)

CHAPTER

# Women Make Great Disciples

THERE WERE SEVERAL INFLUENTIAL WOMEN IN
the Bible, but one in particular comes to my mind. In the book
of John, Chapter 4, John didn't mention her name, but he said she
was a Samaritan woman. She went to draw water and met Jesus
for the first time. It was the hottest part of the day and He asked
her for some water. Actually He wanted her to ask Him for some
living water, water that would "become in Him a spring of water
welling up to eternal life." John 4:14. Jews did not associate with
Samaritans at that time, but He knew everything about her. She
first thought He might be a prophet after He told her all about
her life, that she had been married five times and the man she was
with was not her husband.

She went on to compare the place of worship for the Samaritans
and the Jews. Jesus' reply was that the location of worship doesn't
matter, "a time is coming and has now come when the true
worshipers will worship the Father in spirit and truth, for they are
the kind of worshipers the Father seeks," John 4:23. God wants
everyone to come to Him with a submissive and obedient heart.

"The woman said, 'I know that Messiah is coming. When He comes He will explain everything to us." "Then Jesus declared, 'I who speak to you am He.' " (This was the first recorded time that He stated who He actually was.) She was so excited and ran back to town and told everyone, " 'Come, see a man who told me everything I ever did. Could this be the Christ?' " John 4:29. This is the man she heard about and waited for all her life, and finally she met Him face to face. The people in town followed her back to the well and were saved that day.

I have heard judgmental remarks from other believers that this woman was a lose sinful woman. It is true, that she had been married five times and with a man she was not married to. Let's look at her life a little closer. First of all, I do not condone sexual relations outside of marriage, but unfortunately that seems to be accepted by many couples today. It doesn't make it right and I know she felt remorse, repented, and was forgiven. Now let's dive into the fact that she was married five times. To those ladies that have been married one time and have or had a wonderful marriage, you will not understand how this could possibly happen to her. But I believe she was trying to do the right thing before God. She said her wedding vows and made the commitment, but it didn't work for unknown reasons. We do not know what the circumstances were that caused the marriages to fail, but suppose the husbands were abusive physically or mentally. Or they were just unequally yoked? Or there could have been family issues that caused the problems? Maybe she had a low self-esteem or maybe she was love- starved as a child and attracted the wrong men in her life? But we do know that she was a believer because she knew about the Messiah and His coming one day. However, she was respected by other Samaritans because they paid attention to her when she told them about her encounter with Jesus. They followed her back and many were saved because of her testimony. She not only lead them physically, but spiritually to Christ. She was forgiven for her past sins and I believe she was obedient to God from that day forward. She, like other women in the Bible, they were instrumental in the Lord's work by spreading the gospel and leading others to Christ. I find them extraordinary disciples and you could be one too. So let's not be quick to judge others when we see only a small portion of their lives. Jesus changes us, changes all of us when we surrender our lives to Him. This is not the end of the story of the Samaritan woman that John wrote about. Oh no, this is just the beginning of her life story by bearing much fruit and witnessing the Lord's harvest.

We all should have a pure clean heart and spirit to have a real intimate relationship with Jesus Christ. But it is only possible through His death and resurrection. It is okay to cry out to God when things are too difficult to handle, but then you need to listen to His instructions through the Holy Spirit. I also believe He wants to hear us say that we forgive those who have wronged us and hand over those grievances to Him. He wants to know that you will trust Him to take care of those who have hurt you and the faith that He will comfort you with peace and shower you with His blessings. It isn't easy to live with injustice, but consider that Jesus is also human and yet never sinned. He has suffered more than we will ever experience. Remember, He never said a word in His defense during His trials, His beatings, and

His crucifixion. He didn't deserve our punishment and yet He willingly took on our sins to pay the sin debt that we owed. He loves us so much that He died for us, He took our place. He paid that debt in full once and for all so we could experience eternal life in heaven. He spared us from judgment and hell where there is continuous flames of fire and gnashing of teeth. Again that sounds like a terrible place to go for all eternity. No second chances after judgment, only God's wrath. It would be sad not to ever see your friends and family ever again. Just think of the consequences if you never shared the gospel with them. They may never hear it from anyone else, so what are you waiting for?

In the article, "God's Purpose in Your Pain," Rick Warren clearly states the purpose of our pain:

> Unbelievers are not nearly as impressed with how we handle prosperity as we handle adversity. Pain is what we have in common with everyone, and how we handle suffering is what gives our witness credibility. None of us can control what happens to us in life, but we can choose whether we waste our pain or learn to use it to help others.

> Instead of asking Why is this happening to me? Let's start asking God two other questions: What do You want me to learn? And Who do You want me to help?

Go now and share the Good News with them and tell them Jesus is coming back soon! Have you done all that God has asked you to do? I know I haven't, but I want my ears tuned into the Holy

Spirit's instructions and I have the faith that everything in my life will fall into place with the Lord's guidance, just as He planned long ago! Are you ready to meet Him Face to face? No one knows the time or place when He returns, so Get Ready! And Be Ready!

To reiterate a page from Charles Stanley's book, (Jesus, Our Perfect Hope, 177) I will get to the reason why I wrote this book, but let me share what Charles had to say about abusive relationships.

> "If you've been abused or mistreated—make a choice right now that you're not going to allow the offender to dictate the course of your life or keep you from doing what God has called you to accomplish."

> "Although behavioral researchers have discovered that those who are wounded by others often go on to repeat the pattern, as Christians, we can choose to be conformed to Christ's image Romans 8:28-29. We can say:

> Lord, I choose to be a loving, forgiving person as Jesus is. So Father, please free me from the wounds I've experienced and transform me into Your likeness. Teach me to be godly, wise, and sacrificially loving as Jesus is. And work through everything I've been through so I can be a more compassionate and effective minister to others. Amen.

Jesus, this is indeed my prayer. Thank you for turning my wounds into a platform of Your victory. Amen."

**"'THE CHRISTIAN LIFE IS MEANT TO BE AN ONGOING PURSUIT OF GOD. TO WALK THROUGH THE DOOR OF SALVATION AND STAND STILL, WITHOUT DRAWING ANY CLOSER TO HIM, IS TO MISS THE TREASURES THAT ARE AVAILABLE IN CHRIST. THOSE WHO SEEK THE LORD WILL SOON DISCOVER THAT KNOWING HIM IS THE GREATEST REWARD OF ALL.'"**

—Dr. Charles Stanley

Well, this brings me to the reason for writing this book. The Lord truly laid it on my heart to write how much God loves each one of us. He had a plan and a purpose to fulfill before we were formed in the womb. That might sound strange, but He created us in His image. Since He is fully God and fully man, He can sympathize with us when we hurt from painful experiences and He can share in our joy when we are happy. My prayer for each of you that you find the peace in God that only He can provide. We do not have to seek attention or self-esteem from others, He is right there in your heart. It has taken me a long time to realize God's plan and purpose for my life and I am a much stronger person because of it. Ladies, this is not the end, but only the beginning of an adventurous and remarkable life when He is the Guide. I'll be Running Home!

Printed in the United States
by Baker & Taylor Publisher Services